Evelyn Glennie

Three Chorales for Marimba

A Little Prayer
Light in Darkness
Giles

My *Three Chorales* for solo marimba were written at different times as individual pieces, and not originally intended as a set to be played together.

A Little Prayer and *Light in Darkness* were written when I was 13 years old, expressing my spiritual feelings and at the same time displaying a pleasantly relaxed dimension of the instrument. *Giles* is dedicated to a friend who was tragically killed in a climbing accident. All three pieces are in simple chorale style and take full advantage of the unique resonance of the marimba.

A Little Prayer is recorded on RCA/BMG RD 60242 (CD,LP & Cassette) and *Light in Darkness* on RCA/BMG RD 60557 (CD only)

THREE CHORALES
A LITTLE PRAYER

EVELYN GLENNIE

© 1994 by Faber Music Ltd.

This music is copyright. Photocopying is illegal.

Move forward
mf
rit.
Tempo primo
pp
mp
mf
f
rit. al fine
pp
niente
Instruments without a low G play these notes an octave higher.

LIGHT IN DARKNESS

Instruments without a low E play these notes an octave higher.

GILES

Five octave marimba
Roll all notes

EVELYN GLENNIE

37 Più mosso
p sub. cresc.
ossia if no low E & D
45
f
53
più f
61
ff
ff
69
pp
niente